PICTURE
WORD BOOK

The images on the cover of this book focus on toys that come alive in children's imaginations—just as words come alive when the magic of reading takes place.

MACMILLAN/McGRAW-HILL

Macmillan/McGraw-Hill School Publishing Company
New York   Chicago   Columbus

Editorial Staff

Editor in Chief	Judith S. Levey
Managing Editor	Helen Margaret Chumbley
Editors	Deirdre Dempsey, Susan R. Norton
Production Manager	Karen L. Tates

Art Staff

Design Director	Zelda Haber
Associate Design Director	Joan Gampert
Art Director	Murray Belsky
Design	Anna Sabin
Artists	Barbara Bash, Karen Baumann, Courtney Studio, Norman Dane, Nancy Didion, Dora Leder, Susan Lexa, Frederick Marvin
Clerical Assistant	David Salinas
Cover Art	Fred Winkowski

Macmillan/McGraw-Hill School Division
866 Third Avenue
New York, New York 10022

Printed in the United States of America

This dictionary is also published in a trade edition
under the title *Macmillan Picture Wordbook*.

ISBN 0-02-195001-6/K-1

9 8 7 6 5 4 3 2 1

A Word To Parents And Teachers About The

Macmillan/McGraw-Hill Picture Word Book

A child's world is filled with spoken and written words. Words in the natural environment such as *Stop, No Parking,* and *Exit* cause children to become aware of the meaning of written language at an early age.

A picture word book extends children's knowledge of language by showing them that words name objects in not only their own environment but also in the larger world.

- When opening the *Macmillan/McGraw-Hill Picture Word Book* for the first time, children will probably want to flip through all the pages, stopping when something special catches their eye. Point out some of the words they may be interested in.

- Listening and talking together while looking at the *Picture Word Book* is important. There are recurring figures of children in the book. Invite children to find these children in several scenes in the book.

- Many of the topics covered in the *Picture Word Book* are classified by place. Help children find the same or similar places in their environments.

Using the *Picture Word Book* to play the games suggested below is a delightful way to discover the variety in the book.

- **I Spy:** As you enjoy the book together, take turns saying "I spy something red," or "I spy something round," or, "I spy something with four legs."

- Category Games such as **Twenty Questions:** Begin by saying: *I'm thinking of something that belongs in a house.* The child then asks questions about the object such as *Does it belong in a kitchen? Do you eat with it?* The questions can only be answered by the word *Yes* or *No*.

- **Word Hunt:** As children become interested in recognizing words, invite them on a Word Hunt. Give them lists of foods to look for that are pictured at the market, for example. See if they can find them in the *Picture Word Book*.

- **Collecting Words** Children may enjoy collecting their favorite words from the *Picture Word Book* and writing them on cards. Or, work with children to make your own picture word book together that has children's choices for the words to be included.

Let the *Macmillan/McGraw-Hill Picture Word Book* be a part of a home or a classroom writing center. Encourage children to use the book during quiet reading or journal writing times. Take it on class or family trips. As children begin to experiment with writing messages and making lists, they may naturally use the *Picture Word Book* for ideas. As they become interested in the spelling of words, encourage them to look to the *Picture Word Book* for help.

For some children, the *Picture Word Book* will be their first reading book. Help children discover a love for and appreciation of language through this introduction to printed words.

Contents

top

bottom

on

off

up

down

out

in

IN THE PARK

grass

jungle gym

bench

slide

tunnel

tree

fountain

swings

merry-go-round

next to

behind

in front of

through

over

under

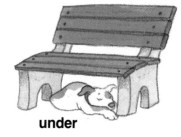

around

IN THE HOME

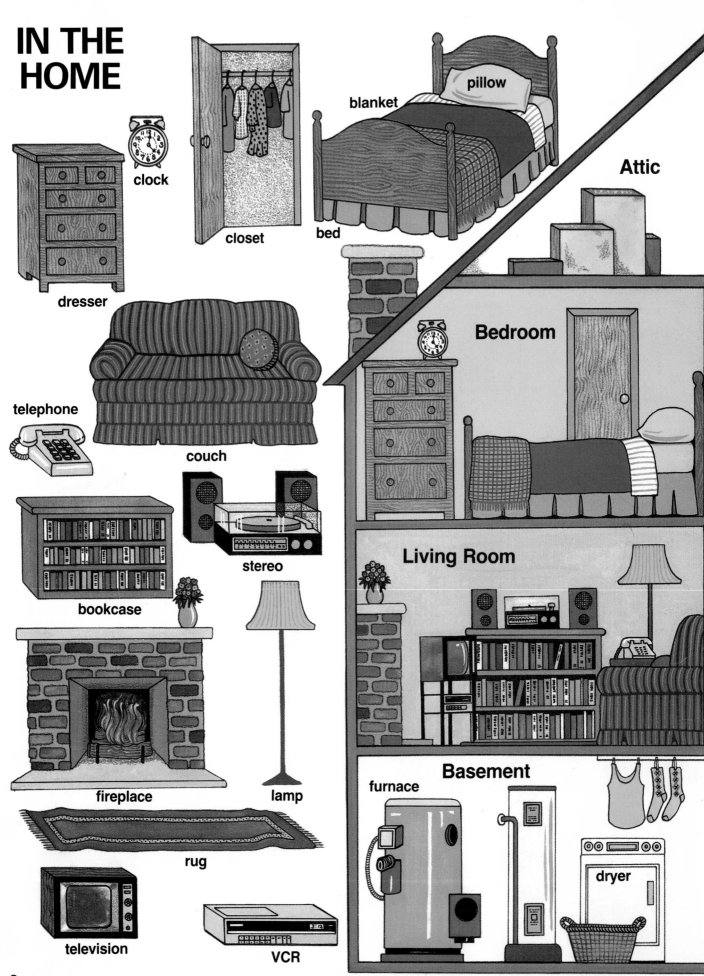

clock

dresser

closet

blanket

pillow

bed

Attic

telephone

couch

Bedroom

bookcase

stereo

Living Room

fireplace

lamp

rug

Basement

furnace

television

VCR

dryer

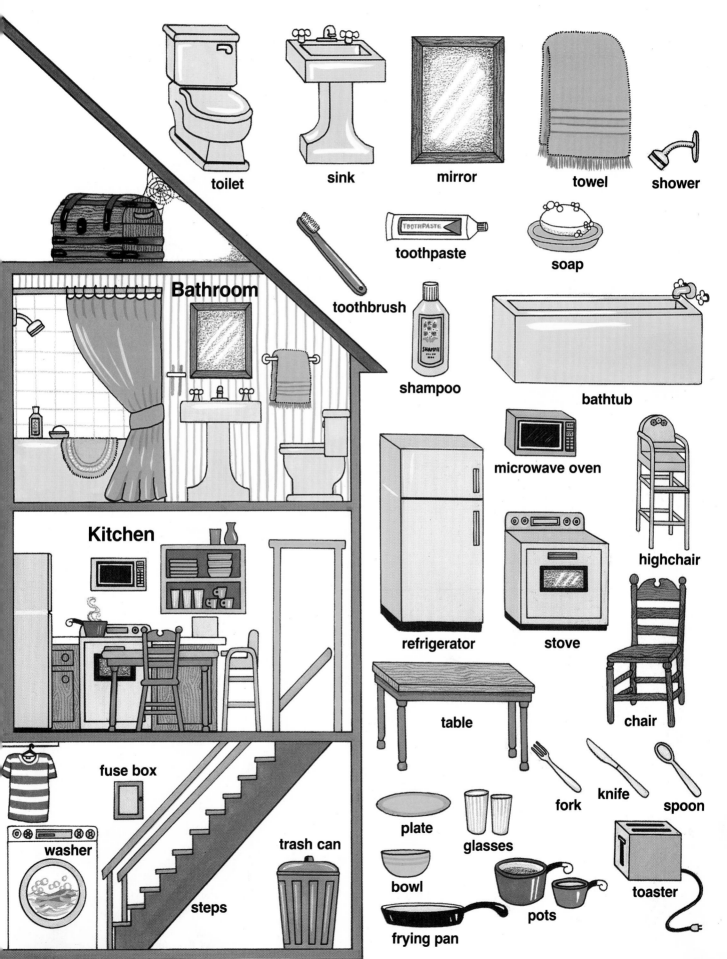

toilet

sink

mirror

towel

shower

toothbrush

toothpaste

soap

Bathroom

shampoo

bathtub

microwave oven

highchair

Kitchen

refrigerator

stove

chair

table

fuse box

knife

fork

spoon

trash can

plate

glasses

washer

toaster

steps

bowl

pots

frying pan

HOMES

town house

two-family house

antenna

chimney

roof

shutter

House

window

door

lawn

mobile home

apartment building

log cabin

tepee

house on stilts

garage

adobe house

driveway

igloo

11

AT SCHOOL

globe

headphones

tape

aquarium

easel

paintbrush

tape recorder

paints

student

paper

scissors

markers

bulletin board

clock

flag

9:00 Shared Reading
9:30 Journal Writing
10:00 Music
10:30 Recess
11:00 Individual Activities

teacher

chalkboard

chalk

eraser

calendar

computer

book

table

chair

abacus

paste

pencil sharpener

crayons

pencil

13

AT THE SUPERMARKET

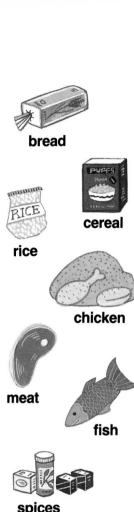

bread

cereal

rice

chicken

meat

fish

spices

cheese

milk

apples

eggs

oranges

grapes

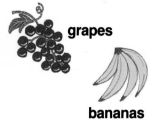

bananas

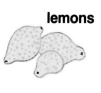

lemons

tomatoes

lettuce

carrots

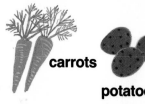

potatoes

street light

school

subway

skyscraper

teleph...
bo...

department ...re

poli...
officer

ta...

bus
stop

parking
garage

church

parking
meter

post office

hospital

library

mailbox

bookstore

movie theater

fire hydrant

grasshopper

butterfly

flowers

parrot

monkey

gorilla

herd

gazelle

rhinoceros

ostrich

hyena

leopard

vines

toucan

tiger

ferns

JUNGLE

20

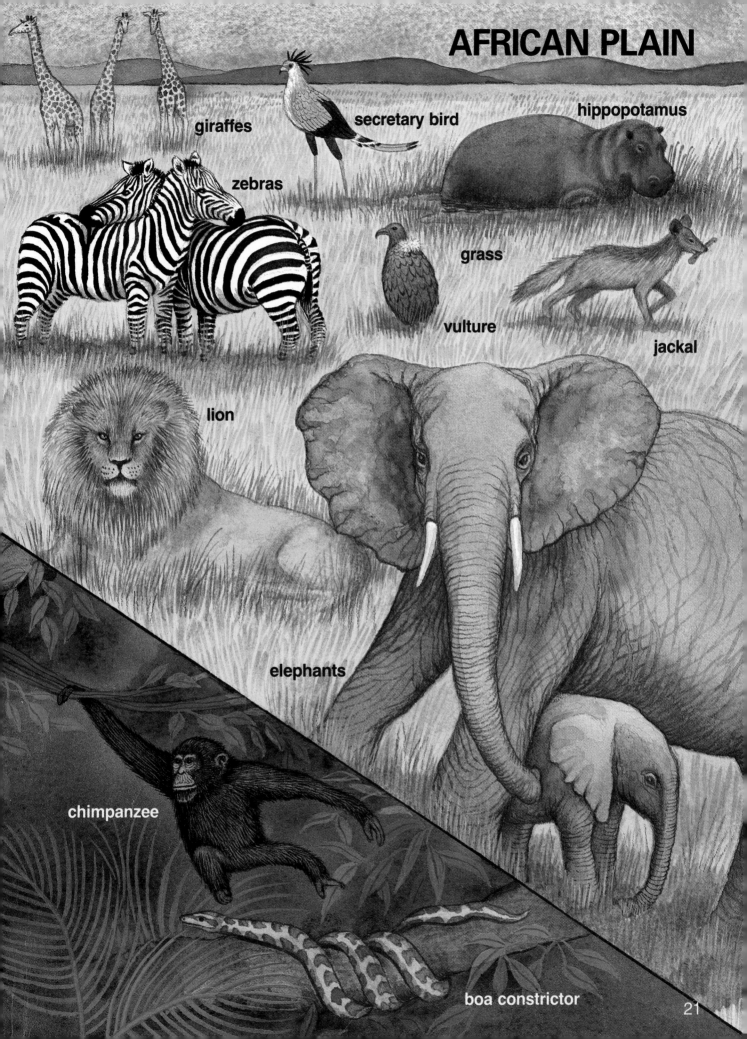

AFRICAN PLAIN

giraffes

secretary bird

hippopotamus

zebras

grass

vulture

jackal

lion

elephants

chimpanzee

boa constrictor

21

DESERT

cactus

mule deer

fox

roadrunner

coyote

burrow

jackrabbit

gila monster

rattlesnake

lizard

spider

mouse

scorpion

MOUNTAINS

peak

valley

eagle

bighorn sheep

mountain goats

waterfall

stream

mountain lion

bear

cave

wildflowers

moss

bats

leaves

acorns

raccoon

pine

owl

oak tree

FOREST

branch

pine cones

porcupine

woodpecker

deer

birch

opossum

rabbit

moose

trunk

violets

skunk

mushrooms

squirrel

chipmunk

caterpillar

24

SWAMP

cypress

mangrove

beaver

flamingos

alligator

cattails

dragonfly

egret

reeds

muskrat

water lilies

frog

turtle

25

POLAR REGIONS

musk ox

reindeer

walruses

ice and snow

ermine

snowy owl

arctic fox

polar bear

arctic hares

sea urchins

dolphin

turtle

sea horse

jellyfish

tuna

26

sky

penguins

flying fish

seals

ocean

crab

starfish

barnacles

mussels

sponges

sea anemone

seaweed

coral

lobster

octopus

eel

swordfish

manta ray

whale

UNDER THE SEA

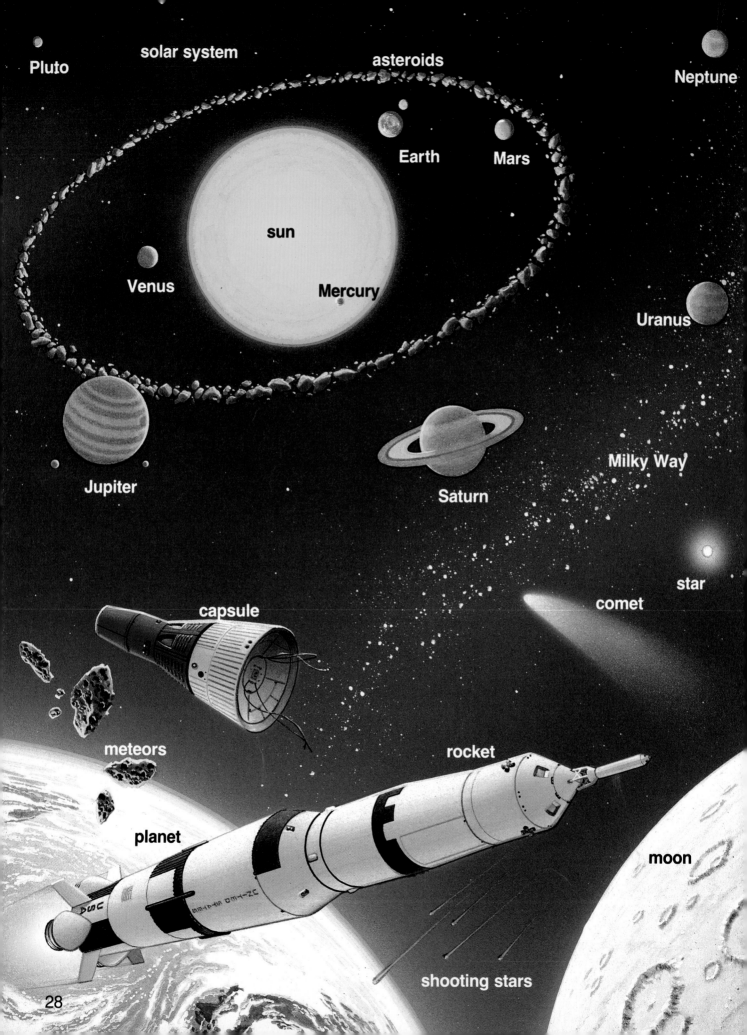

Pluto

solar system

asteroids

Neptune

Earth

Mars

sun

Venus

Mercury

Uranus

Jupiter

Saturn

Milky Way

star

comet

capsule

meteors

rocket

planet

moon

shooting stars

OUTER SPACE

space stations

satellite

spacesuit

lunar module

astronaut

space shuttle

SPRING

hill

flying a kite

hiking

playing baseball

pond

ducks

fishing

mowing the grass

jogging

riding a bicycle

roller-skating

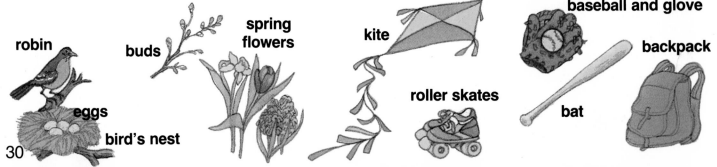

robin

buds

spring flowers

kite

baseball and glove

roller skates

bat

backpack

eggs

bird's nest

SUMMER

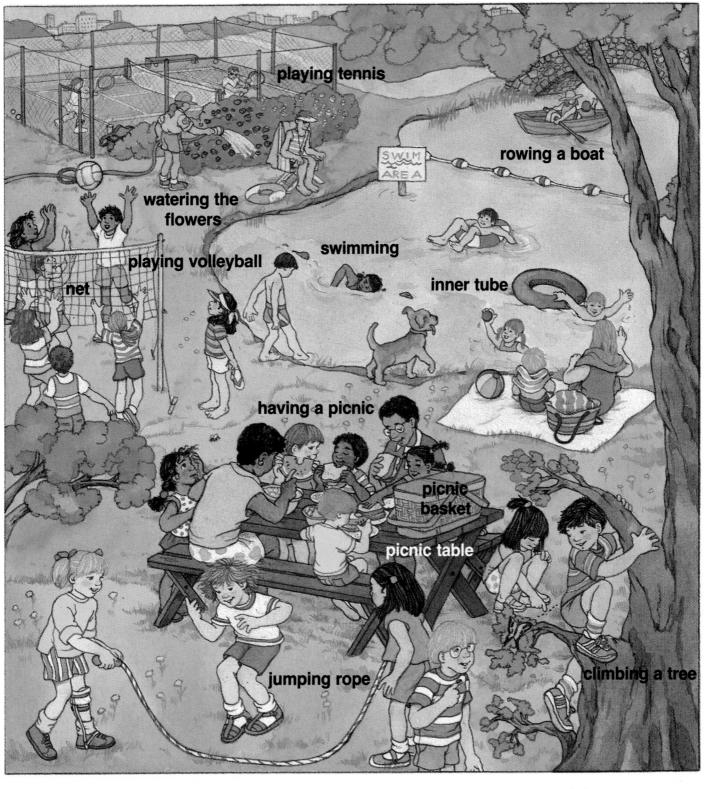

playing tennis

rowing a boat

watering the flowers

SWIM AREA

swimming

playing volleyball

inner tube

net

having a picnic

picnic basket

picnic table

jumping rope

climbing a tree

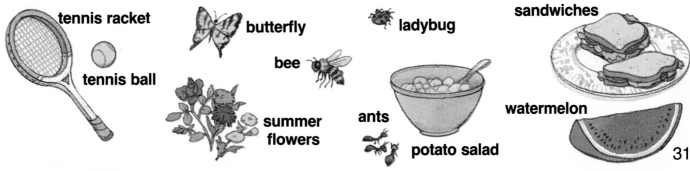

tennis racket

butterfly

ladybug

sandwiches

tennis ball

bee

summer flowers

ants

potato salad

watermelon

31

FALL

playing soccer

hay

going on a hayride

wagon

raking leaves

carving pumpkins

picking apples

ladder

apples

cider

pumpkin

soccer shoes

geese

squirrel

rake

basket

soccer ball

acorns

skiing

sledding

holly bush

playing ice hockey

shoveling snow

ice-skating

ice

bird feeder

making a snowman

making snow angels

making snowballs

evergreen tree

sled

ski poles

skis

ice skates

hockey stick

hockey puck

cardinal

sparrows

holly leaves and berries

icicles

33

CLOTHES WE WEAR

cloud
umbrella
rain hat
rain
raincoat
poncho
rain boots
puddle

A Rainy Day

lifeguard
sun
sunglasses
T-shirt
shorts
sun hat
bathing suit
sneakers
sand
sandals

A Sunny Day

cap
jeans
dress
socks
jacket
pants
sweater
pajamas

snow

earmuffs

hat

mittens

gloves

snowsuit

scarf

snowman

parka

snow boots

A Snowy Day

sweatshirt

suspenders

shirt

skirt

coat

sweatpants

nightgown

slippers

shoes

AT THE AIRPORT

runway

cockpit

cabin

jet engine

Airplane

tail

nose

wing

NEWSSTAND

RESTAURANT

baggage truck

flight attendants

GATE 5

gate

waiting area

check-in counter

boarding ramp

control tower

mechanic

baggage compartment

pilot

landing gear

passengers

observation
area

GIFT SHOP

GATES
5-10

rest rooms

arrival and departure
monitors

ticket
agent

INFORMATION

ticket
counter

information desk

275

baggage
carousel

security check

metal detector

boarding pass

garment
bag

carry-on
luggage

skycap

baggage
cart

suitcases

37

TRAINS

tunnel

tank car

steam locomotive

livestock car

switch tower

caboose

Rio Grande

4065

dining car

passenger car

diesel locomotive

railroad crossing

traffic signal

rail switch

bench

crossing gate

engineer

passengers

conductor

porter

trestle

refrigerator car

automobile car

·L·G·B· 4059

boxcar

flatcar

·2·G·B·

D&RGW 4060

sleeping car

267

TRAIN STATION

TAXI

TICKETS

MAP

COFFEE

TAXI

platform

train
signal

TICKETS

tracks

ties

TAXI

stationmaster

waiting room

ticket window

rails

taxi
station

39

AT THE HARBOR

tugboat

barge

flag

buoy

freighter

lifeboat

container truck

motorboat

oars

dock

rowboat

canoe

hull

outboard motor

BOAT HOUSE

40

GOING PLACES

trailer truck

PAY TOLL I MILE

SPEED LIMIT 30

car

bus

ONE WAY

school bus

STOP

NO PARKING

SCHOOL CROSSING

fire engine

jeep

DO NOT ENTER

NO U TURN

43

AT A CONSTRUCTION SITE

beam

crane

girder

scaffold

ladder

lumber

forklift

electrical cables

jackhammer

hand truck

44

power shovel

dumptruck

bulldozer

cement mixer

cement

worker

steamroller

hard hat

shovel

goggles

blowtorch

wheelbarrow

welder

pipes

lunch box

45

wrenches

saw

hacksaw

coping saw

try square

level

hammer

masking tape

safety knife

hand drill

stapler

sledgehammer

vise

sawhorse

tool box

46

WORKING WITH TOOLS

paint brush

jigsaw

paint tray

drill press

electric drill

paint roller

clamps

drill bits

tape measure

screwdrivers

pliers

wire cutters

plane

ruler

circular saw

glue

paint

screws

bolts

nuts

nails

file

sandpaper

drop cloth

47

MAKING MUSIC

harp

triangle

Chorus

piano

sheet music

singer

bagpipe

tambourine

trombone

maracas

guitar

xylophone

saxophone

harmonica

Orchestra

clarinet

tuba

cymbals

French horn

oboe

bass

baton

violin

trumpet

flute

conductor

music stand

cello

bugle

recorder

piccolo

accordion

drum

A FAMILY ALBUM

me

my mother and father

my sister and brother

my mother and her
parents

my grandmother and grandfather and me

my mother and her
brother

my uncle and me

my dog Winky

my father and his sister

my aunt, her daughter and son, and their stepfather

my parents and their niece and nephew

my cousins and me

all of us ♡

VISITING THE DOCTOR

doctor

stethoscope

scale

gauze pads
cotton balls
tongue depressors
bandages

bulb syringe   tweezers   thermometer

blood pressure cuff

nurse

doctor's bag

examining table

patient

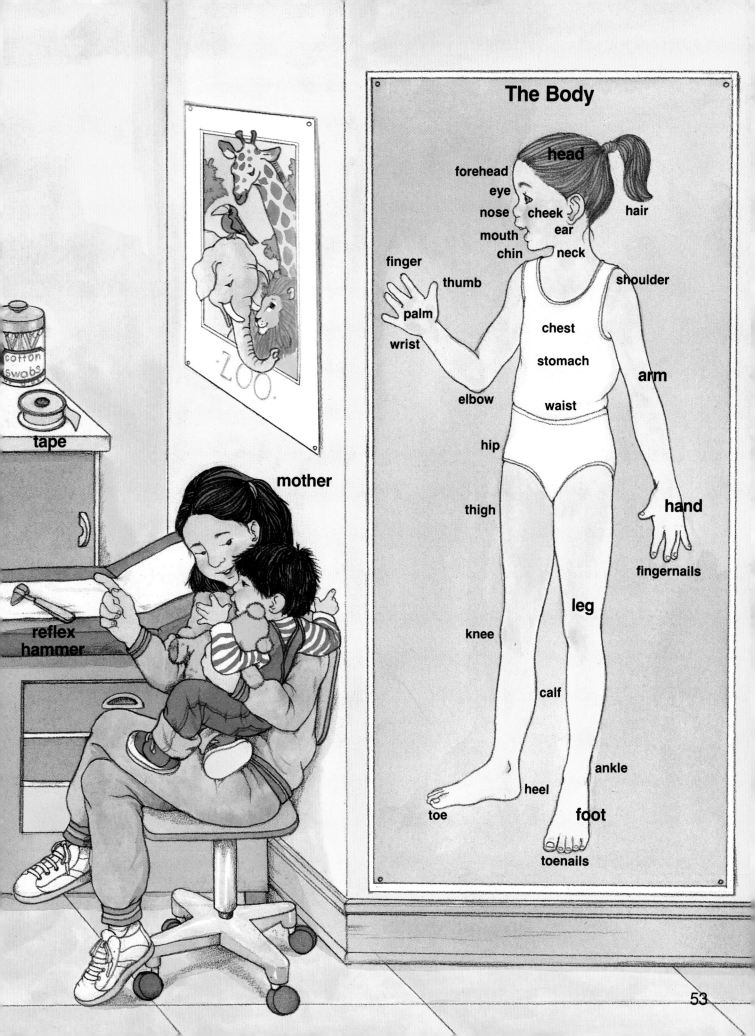

The Body

head
forehead
eye
nose   cheek
mouth   ear   hair
chin   neck
finger
thumb   shoulder
palm
wrist   chest
stomach   arm
elbow   waist
hip
thigh   hand
knee   fingernails
leg
calf
ankle
heel
toe   foot
toenails

cotton swabs

tape

reflex hammer

mother

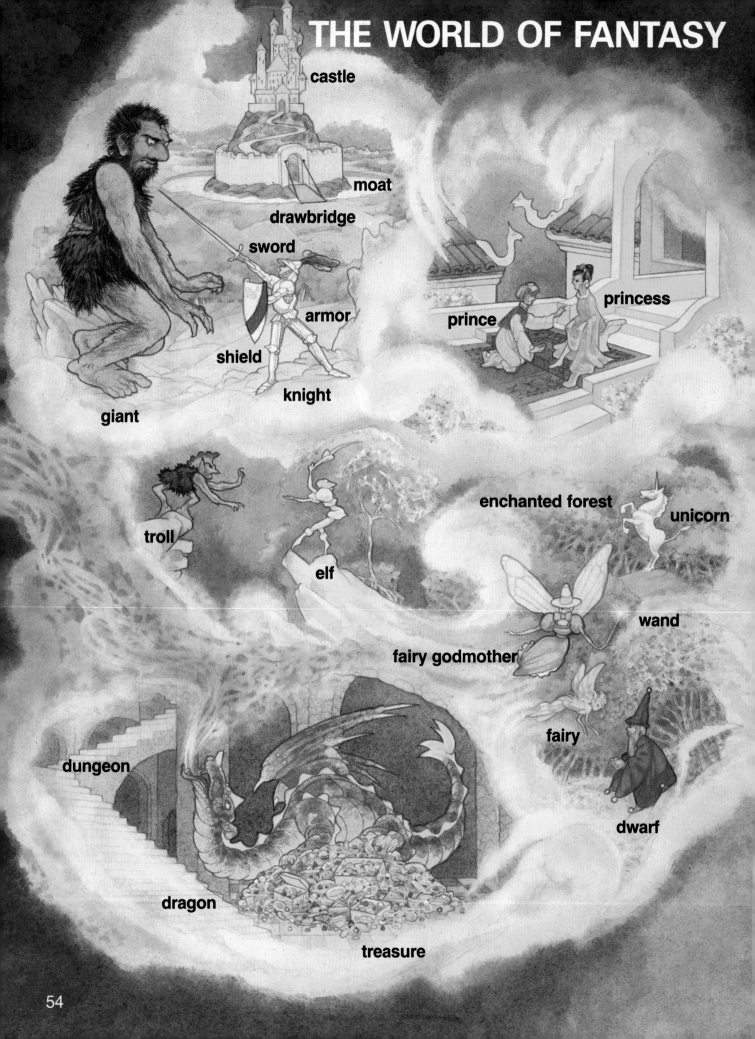

THE WORLD OF FANTASY

castle

moat

drawbridge

sword

armor

shield

knight

giant

prince

princess

troll

elf

enchanted forest

unicorn

wand

fairy godmother

fairy

dungeon

dragon

dwarf

treasure

54

flags

crow's nest

sails

magic carpet

pirate ship

genie

crown

king

queen

wizard

staff

lamp

NUMBERS, OPPOSITES, AND SHAPES

1 one

2 two

3 three

4 four

5 five

6 six

7 seven

8 eight

9 nine

10 ten

many

tall

short

few

high

low

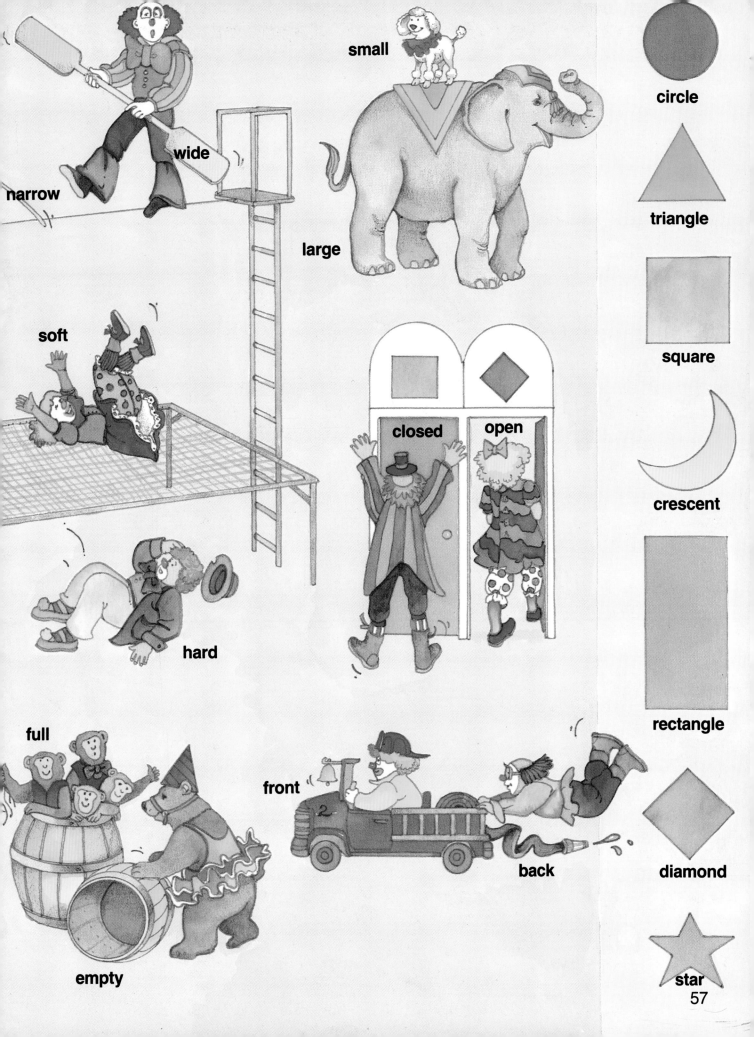

narrow

wide

small

large

circle

triangle

square

soft

closed

open

crescent

hard

rectangle

full

front

back

diamond

empty

star

57

THE ALPHABET AND COLORS

Aa Bb

white

Cc Dd Ee Ff

pink

Gg Hh Ii Jj Kk

red

Ll Mm Nn Oo

orange

Pp Qq Rr Ss

Tt Uu Vv Ww

yellow

Xx Yy Zz

58

green   blue   purple   brown   gray   black

WORD LIST